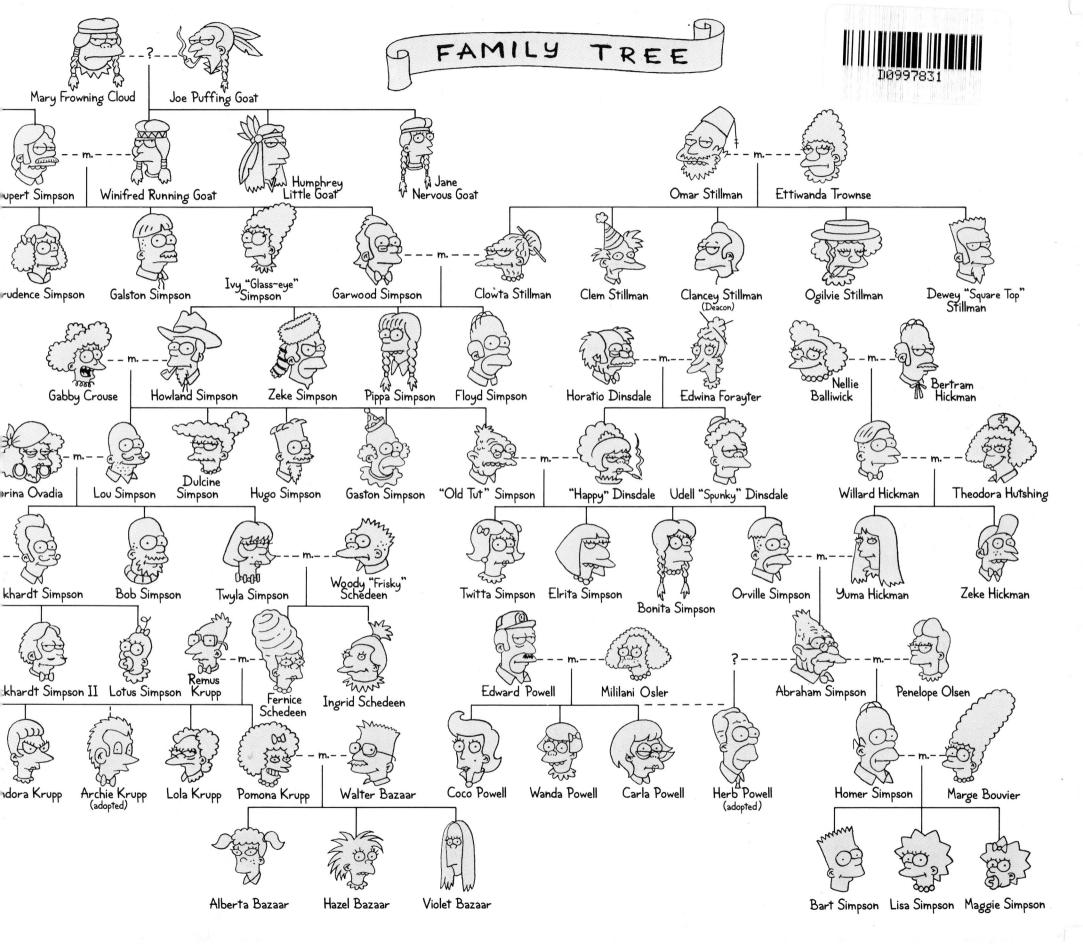

FAMILY TREE

Dedicated to the memory of Snowball I:

We've re-upholstered the couch you shredded, but not our love for you.

THE SIMPSONS™ UNCENSORED FAMILY ALBUM

Published by HarperCollins*Publishers* 1997
77-85 Fulham Palace Road, London W6 8JB
1 3 5 7 9 8 6 4 2

First published in the USA by HarperCollins Publishers Inc, 1991

For information, address HarperCollinsPublishers,
77-85 Fulham Palace Road, London W6 8JB

ISBN 0 00 653018 4

Printed in Great Britain by Scotprint Ltd., Musselburgh

A catalogue record for this book is available from the British Library

Concepts and Art Direction: Mili Smythe
Family Album Chroniclers: Mary Trainor, Ted Brock
Design: Peter Alexander Design Associate: Barbara McAdams
Production Assistance: Kim Llewellyn, Dan Chavira
Creative Team: John Adam, Dale Hendrickson, Ray Johnson, Bill "Babe" Morrison
Willardson & Associates
Chronicle Contributor: Jamie Angell
Editor: Wendy Wolf Legal Advisor: Susan Grode
Typesetting: Skil-Set Graphics

MATT GROENING'S

tHe SIMPSONS™
Uncensored Family Album

HarperCollins*Publishers*

Patty and Selma in their infancy, with our cat, Squirmy.

Patty, Selma (age 3½) and Squirmy.

My first book! In the end, the Li'l Gnome grows to be 9 ft. tall. It taught me a valuable lesson about patience, hope and growth!

My first tooth 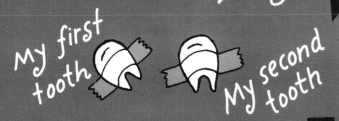 My second tooth

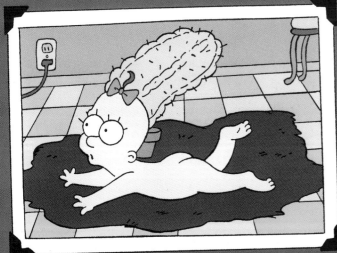

Little Marjorie Bouvier

OOH-WEE!

Despite my handicap, I won the kindergarten apple-bobbing contest.

A "HEY, YOU! READ ME A STORY" BOOK

The **Fuzzy** Li'l **Gnome**
...And how he grew

Before ↓

After ↓

to Marge

your pal, Bruce

My first boyfriend, Bruce Udelhofen

The day I straightened my hair (age 13).

Springfield High School

Certificate of Distinction

Awarded to: *Marge Bouvier*

In recognition of: *"Johnny, We Hardly Heard Ye"*

In the Category: *Dramatic Interpretation*

2ⁿᵈ Place FORENSICS TEAM

Christina Marcello
Supervisor, Springfield School District

Seymour Skinner
Principal, Springfield High School

The Speech I Imagine JFK Would Have Made
At Our Graduation (Had H e Lived)

My fellow citizens of Springfield High, the trumpet

summons us again toa long twilight struggle. THe

torch has been passed to your generation and the

glowfrom that fire can truly light the campus.

So let us Begin.

Ich bin ein Springfielder!

AXXMXXX Ask not what you can do for Spring-

field High, but what Springfield High can do for you..

Other way around?

The first draft of my award-winning dramatic interpretation

Artie Ziff took first place with his poignant reading of "Don't Rain on My Parade", from "Funny Girl."

Springfield Shopper
314 Dutch Elm St.
Springfield

Dear Shopper Editor,

I/I̶'̶v̶e̶ have had it up to here with your "news-
paper" and it's reckless, anti-social policy
of publishing story afterstory of babies
being born, picture after picture of babies,
advertisements of baby products, etc.

Where will it all end?

What about the rest of us who aren̶'̶t̶ not babies?
Did it ever occur to you that we are the
majority? If you ask me, you are only getting
yourself in a real mess because the people
will see all these babby stories and think
"That's a good way to get my name in the
paper," and that only leads to more babies!

So I'm w̶a̶r̶e̶ warning you: if you continue this
policy, I will see to it that no child of
mine ever lays an eye on your publication.

Sicnerely,

Abraham Simpson

Abraham Simpson

P.S. If you don't think I'm serious, you
should see my newborn son. He shows no
interest in what your paper, or anything else
for that matter, has to say. More power to
him if you ask me!

Grandpa's first-recorded letter
of complaint

Little Homer
Simpson, age
3 months

Grandpa's 7,587th
oyster ↓

SHUCKS, He's the World's Best!
By Merl Merlow,
Shopper Business Editor

The Springfield Oyster Shucking Co.
was all abuzz Friday with the news that

Abe Simpson

Abraham Simpson, 29, had hand-
shucked 7,587 oysters between 8:00
Monday morning and 5:00 Friday
afternoon.

Simpson's achievement surpassed the
previous one-week record of 7,428, set
by the late Lud "Load" Dennison in 1943.

"Not to take anything away from Lud
or his beautiful widow," said an elated
Abe Simpson when presented with a
handsome scroll commemorating his
feat, "but you have to remember that the
Load set the record in a six-day work
week during the war, when the only
thing this place turned out was beef in a
tin.

"I'd like to see [Dennison] try to break
5,000, let alone come close to my record,
with big jumbos and those pretty little
ones sailing down the conveyor belt.
Now *that's* shuckin'."

Simpson said he planned to celebrate
quietly at home with his 3-month-old son
Homer.

"I'll probably just relax in front of the
radio and try to get the smell off my
hands," Simpson said.

In other business news... C.
Montgomery Burns, 23, purchased the
run down Springfield Gas and Electric
Co., which has been closed for the past

C. Montgomery Burns

five weeks. When asked whether he
would reinstate the "Lights Out for the
Weekend" campaign, Burns said,"By the
time I'm through, there'll be enough
power around here to light up four or
five Springfields!"

Homer always did have a fondness for donuts.

Grandpa and Homer in happier days.

The first sign of Homer's budding intelligence. I can't really say his handwriting has improved much over the years.

HOMER

The happier days were over quite quickly.

PLEASE DON'T FEED THE ANIMALS

REPORT CARD

Simpson, Homer GRADE 4

SUBJECT	1ST QUARTER	2ND QUARTER	3RD QUARTER	4TH QUARTER	SUMMER-SCHOOL
MATH	D	D	D-	D-	F
ENG	D+	D	D-	F+	F
HIST	D	D+	D+	D-	F
SCI	D-	D-	F	D-	F
GYM	C-	C-	D	D+	D-
ATTEN-DANCE	F	D-	F	D-	F
CITIZEN-SHIP	F	D-	D-	F	D-

NOTES *We would like to hold Homer back a year, but his 4th grade teacher, Mrs. Harvell, has refused to take him back.—HH*

an insult to ... *disruption* *"underachie...*

Our only photo of Herb Powell, Homer's once-wealthy half-brother.

Dear Principal Hartly,
Please excuse Homer's absince of Nov. 8-10. He had to stay home to look after his fathre, who was nearly blinded when he reached to a high shelf and took down a bottle of cleanser he was going to use to clean his medal for the Veterins Day Parade and the cleansr spilled in his face.
Signed,

HOMER'S DAD

Homer on Halloween, in his all-time favorite costume. (age four)

Homer at the tender age of ten. That's Barney Gumble on the left.

Dear Dad,
I'll do anything you say, just don't send me to military school. Please please please please please please pledse please please please.
Your devotid son,
Homer
P.S. Remember. Today is the First day of the rest of your life.

AWARD
Nice Try
WOODSHOP
FOR EFFORT

SIMPSON, H.

Homer's sophomore wood shop project - his first initial. He planned to finish the "J" as a junior and the "S" as a senior.

FROM THE DESK OF
Harlan Dondelinger

To: Abraham Simpson

From: Harlan Dondelinger
Vice Principal

Dear Mr. Simpson:
   I need to talk with you about ways to improve Homer's study habits. His constant efforts to draw attention to himself with noises imitating bodily functions and his off-color attempts at humor during class time have reached the point where I have no alternative but to warn you that drastic measures may be necessary. We've told him repeatedly that he's an underachiever, but Homer seems to think that's a compliment.

Sincerely,
Harlan Dondelinger
Vice Principal

Yours truly!

Mrs. Harvell ← 4th   SPRINGFIELD ELEMENTARY
Mrs. Harvell
Barney!

Principal Hartley

KARMEL KORN

Enjoy the Movie!
Visit the Snack Bar!

DO NOT ATTEMPT TO CHEW UNPOPPED KORN KERNELS.
WE CANNOT BE RESPONSIBLE FOR
BROKEN TEETH OR DENTAL WORK OF ANY KIND.

From when I saw "The Love People" for the 8th time! I wept openly during the deathbed sequence every time!

LiVE!
IT'S A FAR OUT HAPPENING
IN A LUNCH TIME CONCERT!

THE LARRY DAVIS EXPERIENCE

IN THE
SPRINGFIELD HIGH
MULTI-PURPOSE ROOM

Thursday, April 12, 1973   Noon til 12:2?

WARNING: PLEASE DO NOT REMOVE FLYERS FROM SCHOOL NOTICE BOARDS

My Hero!

à mon cher Homer - L'amour, Marge.

The first and last pack of cigarettes I ever bought ↓

LADY Laramie
HI-TAR

"You'll love 'em, Lady!"

Patty and Selma still smoke them! ↑

HANDWRITING ANALYSIS

Your *Personality Revealed Through Penmanship!*

SIGNATURE ___*Marge Bouvier*___

Your signature indicates a sensitive, free-spirited and creative nature. The graceful calligraphic curvatures of your capital letters reveal a love of poetry and music. You are destined for a life of elegance, refinement and artistic fulfillment.

SIGNATURE ___HOMER SIMPSON___

Your signature exhibits a strong tendency toward slackness, inattention and woolgathering. The unsophisticated arrangement of ill-formed lines and circles which comprise your writing suggests an obtuse and insipid outlook. You are doomed to a life of banality, dullness and lethargy.

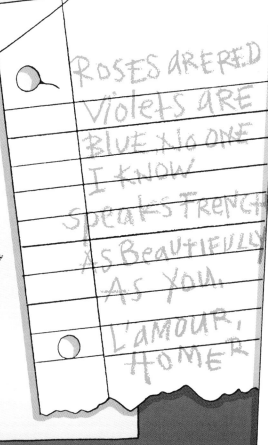

ROSES ARE RED
Violets ARE
BLUE NO ONE
I KNOW
SPEAKS FRENCH
AS BEAUTIFULLY
AS YOU.
L'AMOUR,
HOMER

My 10 favorite Bands of all time, 1973

1. Ringo Starr
2. The Beatles
3. The Larry Davis Experience
4. The Happies
5. Elf Gravy
6. Don Donnally and Jo-Jo

7. Beatlemania
8. The Twigs of Sister Tomorrow
9. The Love Buckets
10. Mr. Funky and the Springfieldians

R.S. + M.B.

Homer's other love— his car ← Such fond memories!

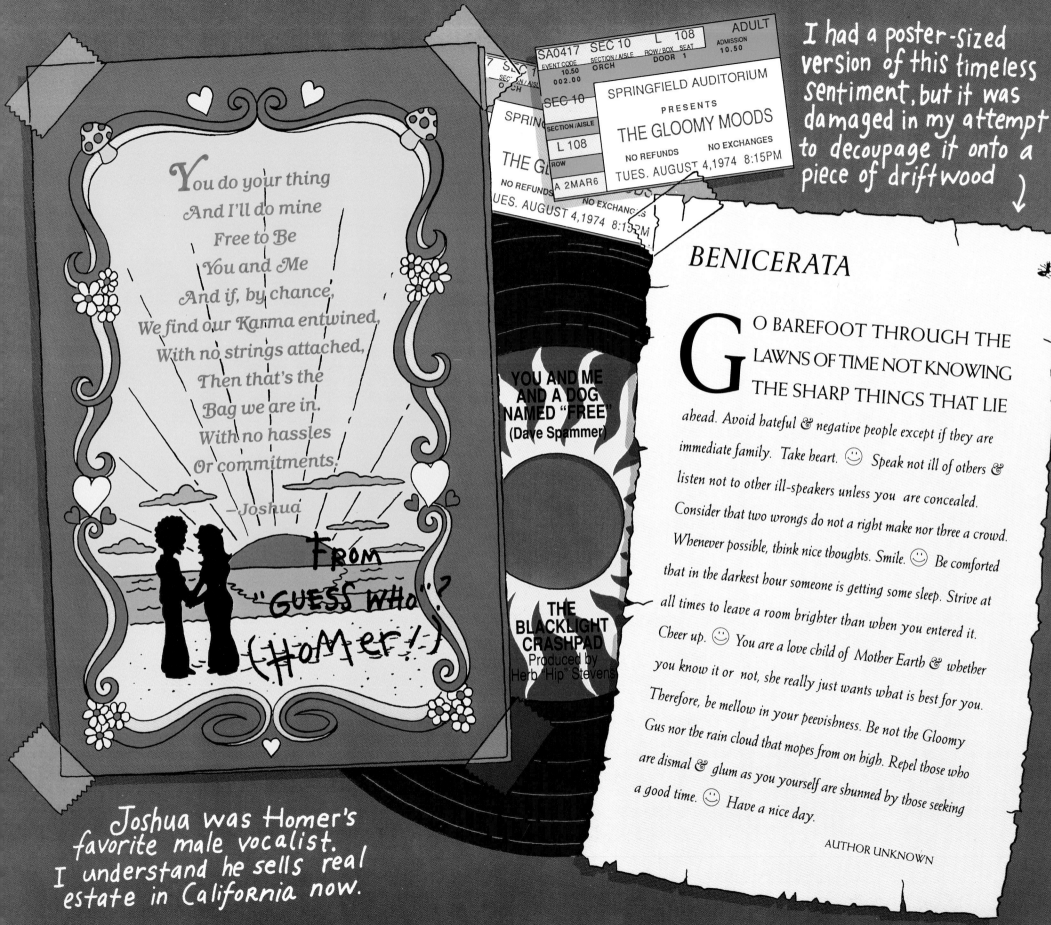

Certificate of Mer...

THIS IS TO CERTIFY THAT

Marjorie Bouvier

has successfully completed the rigorous curriculum of th...
Springfield Unified School District and is hereby deeme...

Excellent

Given this ___16th___ Day of ___June___ ,
Nineteen Hundred and ___74___ .

Grace Vitale

Supervisor, Springfield Unified School District

Principal, Springfield High Sc...

Certificate of Merit

THIS IS TO CERTIFY THAT

Homer Simpson

has successfully completed the rigorous curriculum of the
Springfield Unified School District and is hereby deemed...

Adequate

Given this ___16th___ Day of ___June___ ,
Nineteen Hundred and ___74___ .

Grace Vitale

Supervisor, Springfield Unified School District

Principal, Springfield High School

The Annual
Senior Class
Graduation
Bonfire and
Weenie
Roast

Homer

KZMK

Cosmic Radio for a More Cosmic Springfield!

WIN A Trip to Beautiful

H A W A I I

JUST BY SENDING US YOUR TOP 10
DESERT ISLAND 8-TRACK CARTRIDGES!

1) "BABY, DON'T Get All Bent out of Shape" - the New Wunkies

2) "Feelin' KINDA Bummed Out" - JOSHUA

3) "Greatest Hits, Vol. 2" - the LARRY Davis Experience

4) "Jesus Was a Hippie" - Original Broadway Cast

5) "Hung Up in Your Macrame" - the Gloomy Moods

6) "Outta Sight, INNA DAZE" - Cosmic Consciousness, Inc.

7) "My Live-in Lady Love" - John Colorado

8) "A decade of OpENING Acts" - One Horse Stagecoach

9) "Just Doin' my Thing", Vol. 3 - Joshua

10) "Also Spracht Zarathustra" - the Electric Orange Dirigible

Name: Homer Simpson
Address: 37½ E. Street, Springfield

* 3 Days and 2 Nights at the exotic Poi Lanai Motel, located on
the secluded Island of Koolawe. Air fare not included.

"DIG" THE "SCENE" AT...

THE LAVA·LAMP A·GO·GO!

SPRINGFIELD'S "GROOVIEST" DISCO!

BIG PAY!
YOU CAN $ STEP UP TO
working in...
NUCLEAR POWER PLANTS
(See Inside Front Cover for Details)
NEXT TO MEL'S WATERBEDS
AND POSTERS EMPORIUM

A souvenir from when Homer and I were "swinging singles"!

Homer's Lucky tee

In our wacky days!

I DIDN'T KNOW they createDA tribute to Dad at Sir Putt-A-Lots

HOLE #9

Marriage Certificate

THIS DOCUMENT CERTIFIES _Marge Bouvier_

AND _Homer Simpson_ TO BE UNITED IN HOLY

MATRIMONY ON THE _29_ DAY OF _September_

BY THE POWERS VESTED (BY LAW) IN A JUSTICE OF THE

PEACE, AT THE _Lucky 7 Wedding Chapel_

Milford A. Alexander
Justice of the Peace

OFFICIANT

Doris Troy
Clerk

"May your marriage not be a lemon."

Our favorite casino!
Such lovely
memories!

The WOODEN NICKEL Saloon & Casino

HEY-
WHAT HAVE
YOU GOT
TO LOSE?!

THIS COUPON ENTITLES
BEARER TO ONE (1)
FREE ALCOHOLIC
BEVERAGE OF CHOICE.
WITH PURCHASE OF $50 IN CHIPS.
Sorry: No Tropical Drinks,
Blended Drinks or Soft Drinks
...rinks or Soft Dri...

THE TOMB OF THE UNKNOWN HITCH-HIKER

A Public Service Cautionary Statue

For the Tub of Your Life
KUSTOM-KRAFTED SPAS AND HOT TUBS
⊙ **Nathen "Red" Wood**
"Not 'Just Another' Spa & Hot Tub Salesman"
24 Hour Beeper: 1-800-555-9007

This grim monument is located on a particularly
desolate stretch of highway not far from the Lucky 7.

We met this nice
man while playing keno.
I found it hard to believe
he was in such a risqué
line of work!

DEAR Ringo,

I hope you like this paINTING I DID
of you. You are my favorite musician in
the universe (really!)

What do you like to eat?
Is your hair really that shape all the time?
Do you have hamburgers and French fries
in England?

Well, that's all for now. Please write me
you have time in your very busy schedule.

Yours truly,

Your biggest fan,

Marge Bouvier :)

Marge Bouvier

(P.S. I am
not a
lunatic.)

Lucky Coin Gelatin Mold

(Whoever gets the coin is Lucky for a day!)

2 packs blue gelatin mix

3 cups "Krusty Brand" corn
sweetener

1 lb. bag multi-colored
"Kitchen Dee-Lite" miniature
marshmallows

1 Lucky coin (for chefs on a budget,
pennies are acceptable. For special
events, try using a Bicentennial
quarter.)

My secret ingredient :

: Fla

Boil gelatin i
Pour into m
Add marshm
Chill for

Voila!

SPRINGFIELD GELATIN COOK-OFF

BOUVIER

THIRD PLACE

August 1980

SPRINGFIELD THIRD PLACE FAIR

For this prize-winning mold, I used an Indian-head nickel! ↑

SPRINGFIELD NUCLEAR POWER PLANT

EMPLOYEE EVALUATION SHEET

Complete the Sentence: The most important thing for any worker is: ___

to try NOT TO LET THE SAME SONG KEEP RUNNING THROUGH YOUR HEAD

Behind my back, friends say I'm: ___ ~~An EASY~~

~~WORTH KNOWING~~ BRAVE, CLEan AND REVEREND.

My ideal dinner would be: ___ **APPROVED**

SMOTHERED WITH COUNTRY GRAVY.

Hom

page 12

NUCLEAR POWER IS OUR BEST FRIEND

S.N.P.P. IDENTIFICATION CARD   1976

NAME: SIMPSON, HOMER
CLASS: SECTOR D
00876-54779-4   *Homer Simpson*

OUR MOTTO: A Tense Workplace is a Productive Workplace

Homer on the morning of his first day of work as a Power Plant employee!

...And at the end of his first day.

Child

Name:
Sex:
Singl
Ethnic
Time:
Place:

Parents

Last Na
Mother's
Place of
Place of

Doctor

Nurse

My special
little guy

Barnacle Bill's

FREE!
Corncob Pipe
with purchase!

HOME PREGNANCY TEST

"Ahoy,
Maties!

If the water turns blue,
a baby for you!

If purple ye see, no baby thar be!

If ye test should fail, to a doctor set sail!"

S P R I N G F I E L D   G E N E R A L
HOSPITAL

Founded 1925   Established 1926

April 2

Dear Mr. and Mrs. Simpson,

After careful consideration and in view of
complaints registered by other parents, we must ask
that you remove your son from the hospital no later
than 5 p.m. today, so that we may ensure the well-
being of the other newborns.

As you usher baby Bert into the world, Dr. Mizzell,
our director of maternity, has asked me to convey to
you the following wish:
Don't bring him back.

Sincerely,

Hilda Beck

Hilda Beck, R.V.N.
Director of Nursing

"Your illness is our business."

5637 Underweather Blvd., Springfield   Right across from the Burns Memorial Golf Course.

CIGAR

EXPLO-DO

BE
THE LIFE OF
THE PARTY

THEY
REALLY
EXPLODE

It was awfully
nice of them to keep Bart in a private room
for the rest of the afternoon.

New Arrivals

WELCOME
Justinian Toby Carson of Springfield. A robust 8 pounds 4 ounces of All-American Boy, and no April Fool! Congratulations from your gushing grandparents—Libby, Big Bill, Viv and Captain Jack.

AIN'T SHE SWEET?!
Ashley Tiffany Hurley Born March 30 to Joe Don and Raelene Hurley of Springfield. Younger than springtime by nine days, honey, but you'll catch up soon enough. From your cousins Jim Bob, Erlene and Buford of Capital City, where all of us Hurleys are in a real hurry to meet you.

TROUBLE AHEAD!
Bartholomew J. Simpson Born April 1 to Homer and Marjorie Simpson of Springfield. A mere 7 pounds 5 ounces of spontaneous combustion, but look what that one little cow did to Chicago. Marge, don't say we didn't warn you. Your loving sisters are close by in case 911 is busy. Patty and Selma. P.S. We saw Artie Ziff the other day and he asked after you. Such a nice boy.

EGG DROP!
Huong Kim Nguyen Born April 2 to Nguyen and Th Nguyen of Springfield. Especially for you, little Nguyen, a birthday haiku:

Lotus child, welcome.
It's a small world after all.
Springfield, have a cow!

From your auntie Kim Tran.

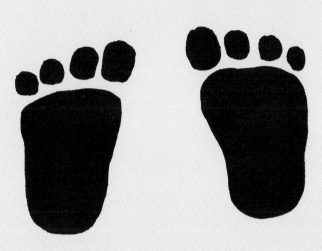

SPRINGFIELD GENERAL HOSPITAL

Name: Simpson, Bartholomew

Parents: Marge/Homer

Date: April 1st

Weight: 7.2 lbs.

Length: 19.0" Sex: ~~X~~ M

Delivering Physician:

Dr. Julius Hibbert

Homer's

← Mine

My first grey hair (and hopefully my last!)

SPRINGFIELD GENERAL HOSPITAL

CLAIMS DEPT.

We regret to inform you that unless the outstanding balance shown below is paid in full by September 15, we will have no alternative but to repossess your child.

Delivery and Maternity Care
Bartholomew J. Simpson
Balance Due: $1,499.99

FINAL NOTICE

BARTHOLOMEW J. SIMP

I was so thrilled when the doctor announced: "four toes on each foot, four fingers on each hand."

Bart and Lisa's first Haircuts.

After

Before

After

Before

Lisa's hair never quite grew back the same.

Spend the night with

ELVISH
(EL-VEESH´)

ELVISH 'N' KABOB!

"THE TURKISH ELVIS"
Enjoy a Most Intimate Spectacle!
An incredible life-like simulation of an actual
Elvis concert re-enactment!
Live, on stage four times a night, seven days a week!
"I get deja-vu everytime I see it!" - Cliff Wilkins
The Town Crier

HUNKA HUNKA BURNIN' KABOB!
Special Dinner 'n' Show Combo.............$27.50
(Includes salad, rolls & choice of beverage or butter)

SIX DRINK MINIMUM ONE

SIX DRINK MINIMUM ONE

We spent
the night with

ELVISH

$17.95 for this STUPID PICTURE!
THEY GET YOU DRUNK THEN THEY
TAKE YOUR MONEY!

Homer at the slots.
He kept saying he "felt lucky", so I couldn't stop him.

Jackpot!

Homer after
he lost the entire
$ 11,158.97

Homer's Shining Hour

HOP-A-LONG'S Chinese Food * Cocktail Lounge *

WOODEN NICKEL CUSTOMER RECIEPT

Room 7 nights.............$940.00
Meals..........$1,628.00
Maid service.....$99.00
Concierge.......$198.00
Laundry Service....$243.00
Room Service....$766.80
In-room Bar-Total....$964.00
Subtotal........$4838.00
Sales Tax.......$241.90
Total.........$5079.90

Needless to say, we could not afford to pay our bill.

These nice men wanted to take Homer for a ride, but I assured them it wasn't necessary.

We spent a few weeks more at the old Wooden Nickel than we'd planned.

Homer doing "the Hustle" atop P.R.

A visit to our state's most wondrous rock formation

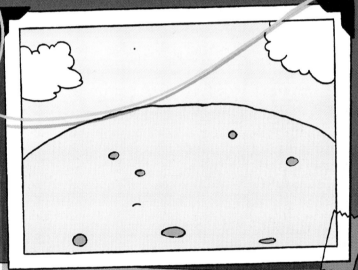

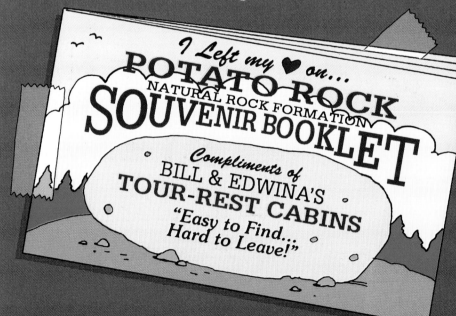

He joked, "Where's the sour cream and chives?" just before he fell off.

Homer was determined not to let this happen again. He bought a new "Liquid Center" ball in the pro shop right afterwards and couldn't wait to try it...

PARTYING DOWN!

Apu donated 76 lbs. of beef jerky to the cause!

HOMER	14	18	29	29	30	38	40	43	45	48	48
BARNEY	20	40	69	87	105	125	151	167	173	203	203

HOMER	10	10	10	16	26	26	38	38	40	49	49
BARNEY	0	0	27	42	51	79	87	107	127	157	157

Homer in Rare Form

Lisa at 22 months. Such a perceptive child!

Yet quite sensitive.

Family Xmas

Snowball I as a kitten. She was cute, but she was BAD!

Springfield kindergarten
REPORT CARD

Name: SIMPSON, LISA
Teacher: MRS. WELLSLEY

Alphabet	A
Storytime	A
Cookies & Milk Time	A
Recess	B
Songtime	A
Numbers	A
	A

Mrs. Simpson,
Lisa is a bright and introspective child. The word "gifted" may be applicable. Although perhaps she is too introspective and gifted for her own good.

Mrs. Wellsley

BART - AGE 8

Bart's first black eye. (and not his last, I'm afraid.)

Lisa with her kindergarten teacher, Mrs. Wellseley. (And her baritone Sax) Age 5.

I had a cat named Snowball --
She died! She died!
Mom said she was sleeping --
She lied! She lied!
Why oh why is my cat dead?
Couldn't that Chrysler hit me instead?
- Lisa Simpson

Here I am pregnant with Little Maggie!

Maggie was such an easy child! By the time she came along, I knew all the tricks!

Maggie's First Birthday

EL BARTO WAS HERE

I was So, so, so proud! ↓

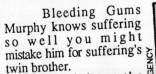

November 4, 1989

Murphy's Tenor Evokes Youthful Anxiety

By Jiff Johnson, *Shopper Music Critic*

Bleeding Gums Murphy knows suffering so well you might mistake him for suffering's twin brother.

Last night at the Jazz Hole, however, Springfield's resident jazzman extraodinaire bent the reed of his tenor sax in the direction of second grader Lisa Simpson.

Murphy introduced the 7-year-old Miss Simpson's composition "The Manipulative Daddy Blues" to an appreciative Hole audience.

What makes this collaboration work is the juxtaposition of Murphy's well-worn (but never tired) voice of experience with the stark, honest perception of Simpson's  youthful dilemma: the need to function in an oppressive home environment while simultaneously yearning for a liberated artistic space.

Murphy's quarte appearing indefinitely Springfield's leading ja venue, continues to brea new ground in this mo American of all music idioms.

ROOTERS NEWS AGENCY

I don't know much about this man's music, but I do wish he'd do something about that name!

The Day Homer Got His New Camera

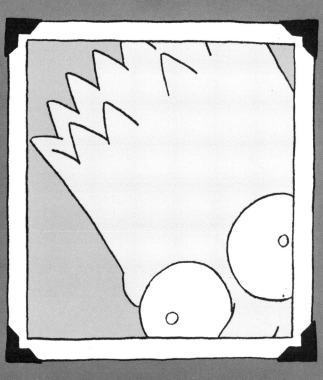

Poem #254

"Optimism" is the thing with fur
That curls upon the sofa
And dreams of Happy Little
        Elves
And never snores -- at all

And in the grimmest hour
        is there --
and annoying though my family be
They cannot bestir the Gentle
        Beast
That keeps my spirit free.

So long I've nurtured it
And thus I'll be repaid.
For it shall, I know it shall
Bring a pony unto me.

Lisa Simpson (age 7)

I didn't even know she had
a pet named "Optimism"!
I just hope it's not some
Sort of rodent.

Maggie's First Step
(well, actually seconds
after her first step)

Maggie's second step

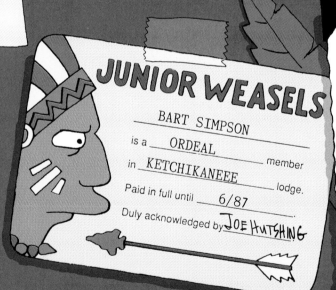

JUNIOR WEASELS

BART SIMPSON

is a ___ORDEAL___ member

in ___KETCHIKANEEE___ lodge.

Paid in full until ___6/87___

Duly acknowledged by JOE HUTSHING

Bart's arrowhead, which he found
at Camp Itchawanda while hunting
for "Snipes".

Luckily, Bart was
a lousy shot.

WARMEST Wishes for a Happy Mother's Day!

MAGGIE   BART

Lisa

COOK _YOUR_ FAVORITE MEAL TONIGHT HONEY! LOVE, HOMER

My lovely Mother's Day card from my loving family...

And my Mother's Day gift from Homer. He explained that he truly believed it's the thought that counts. (Hmm.)

Dumb Things I Gotta Do Today...

Shopping List
1. frozen pork chops
2. (Jumbo Pack)
3. Frosty Krusty Flakes
4. Happy Little Elf Cereal
5. 10 lb. bag of sugar
6.
7. Gelatin Mix (12-pack)

11. Pork Rinds Lite
12. Stuff-itz
13. Kitty Krunchies
14. Yummy Cupcake Mix
15. Xtra-Gritty Lard Peanut butter
16. Diet Brownies
17.
18. Duff Beer (don't forget coupon!)
19.

SPRINGFIELD RETIREMENT CASTLE

To; Advertisers
KLMP Tv
Springfield

DEAR Advertisers,
    I am disgusted with the way old people are depicted on television. We are not all vibrant, fun-loving sex maniacs. Many of us are bitter, resentful individuals who remember the good old days when entertainment was bland and inoffenseive. The following is a list of words I never want to hear on television again. Number one; Bra. Number two; Horny. Number three; Family jewels.

Sincerely yours,
Abrahdm Simpson
Grandpa Simpson

Grandpa Strikes again!

Memories of a vacation Homer would like to forget

Patty and Selma said the resorts of the Devil's Hell-Hole region are the playgrounds of the rich and famous. But I can't imagine rich people wanting to be so darned uncomfortably hot and sweaty!

89¢

GENUINE! DEVIL'S HELL-HOLE SA

Maggie with cow skull.

This snake was actually quite harmless. The proprietor explained he was just being "affectionate."

The Cacti of Mystery

Lisa loved this quaint roadside inn because they had a jukebox filled with scratchy old blues records.

Our "Second Honeymoon"!

(Cut short by a most unfortunate accident.)

Greetings from *SPRINGFIELD*

Home of the Springfield Nuclear Power Plant!

In hopes of a profitable New Year!

I'm watching you - C. Montgomery Burns

Homer's Car!

HOMER SIMPSON

SPRINGFIELD ISOTOPES

H

MASCOT

DANCIN' HOMER SIMPSON

Took the baseball world by surprise in May 1990 when his spontaneous "Baby Elephant Walk" routine during Family Night became the talk of Springfield... Popular appeal earned him a shot at the majors, but "Walk" failed to catch on with Capital City fans...Among mascots, shares record (with several others) for shortest major league career.

HEIGHT: 5'9" **WT:** 239 lbs. **AGE:** 35

LITTLE KNOWN FACT: Homer was named Springfield Nuclear Power Plant "Toxic Waste Handler of the Month" in November, 1986.

"KEEP ONE EYE... ON THE OTHER GUY."

PEER OBSERVATION PROGRAM

OFFENDING EMPLOYEE: Homer Simpson
DATE OF OFFENSE: 8-4-85
TIME OF OFFENSE: All Day

Feel free to check as many offenses as you like. Every effort will be made to keep accuser's name confidential, but management cannot be responsible for leaked information.

EMPLOYEE HAS BEEN SEEN OR HEARD:

✓ taking a nap of more than 15 minutes while opperationg equipment
✓ taking fissionable matieral home for personal use
✓ taking Mr. Burns' name in vain
✓ taking liberties
✓ other (use back of card to describe)

SIGNED (optional): Anonymous

Thank you for helping make the plant more productive.

(Please do not fill out this form on company time.)

A Simpson on a trading card – I never thought I'd see the day!

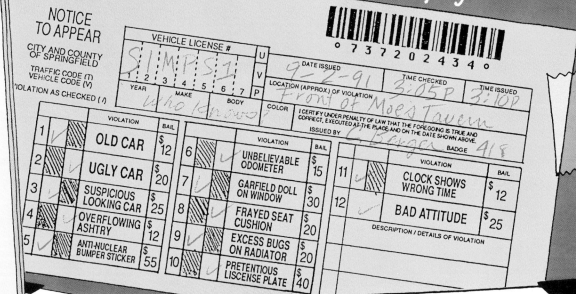

The ticket Homer refused to pay. He said it was a "principal thing" and hung it on the refrigerator.

So later, Police Chief Wiggum and Eddie had to serve Homer with a warrant.

So much for matters of principal!

MOTH

Needless to say, it bounced.
↓

BARNEY GUMBEL
466 Prunetree Ln.
Springfield

00249

Saturday , 1990

Pay ONE MILLION DOLLARS and 00/100

to the Order of HOMER SIMPSON

FIRST NATIONAL BANK OF
SPRINGFIELD, MAIN BRANCH

For BAR BET

Barney Gumbel

Bart's tattoo.
What a frightening
experience! We
had it removed
immediately.

SUNDAY BOB PICKER'S
AMERICA, U.S.A.
NUCLEAR WARHEAD MUSEUM
AND RELIGIOUS ARTS CENTER

FAT MAN

WAY 99 - EAST OF I-385

Ned and Maude
F. sent us this
one. On the
back it reads:
"Pray for peace,
prepare for war,
and vicey-versa!" That
certainly is food for thought!

LIONEL HUTZ
ATTORNEY AT LAW

AS SEEN ON TV!

KLondike 5-LAWW
No Case Too Small!   Se Habla Espanol!
CLOGGING OUR COURTS SINCE 1976

Mambo
your way to
Happiness!

the
Walt Bingham
Way!

Even if you've got two
LEFT feet, we'll put
you on the RIGHT
path! So...don't get
LEFT behind! Start
our classes RIGHT
away before we fill up!

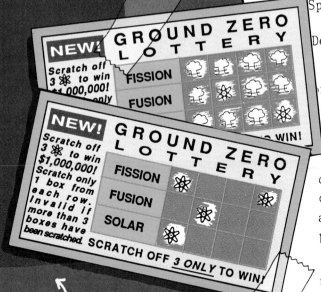

Quality Candles
1954 Burns Parkway
Springfield

Dear Sir or Madam:

Correct me if I'm wrong, but I thought a person's 80th birthday was supposed to be a festive and dignified event.

I don't seem to hear you correcting me.

All right then, how do you suppose I felt when it was time to blow out the Quality (Hah! Now that's a hot one - if you get my meaning) Candle on my 80th birthday cake and I blew my damnedest and nothing happened. Oh, all right, maybe the flame did lean over a few degrees, but not so's you'd notice.

Tell me this, Mr. or Ms. rocket scientist. If I made a wish, and the candle didn't go out, do I get a bonus wish? Well, if I do, here it is: I wish your whole ball of wax would go up in smoke!

Smoldering mad,

Abraham Simpson
Abraham Simpson

P.S. Have you ever thought about making half-size birthday candles? It would save valuable time while honest people such as myself waited for the thing to burn to the ... And another thing - how about chocolate-flavored ... at pink stuff tastes awful!

Bart naked on a bear skin rug.

EL BARTO WAS HERE

Grandpa's 80th Birthday

ANYTHING BUT A SNOOZER!

By Geraldine Meekar-Lyones, *Shopper Book Editor*

AND THEN THEY TOOK NAPS

By Helen Lovejoy
(Tattleton Press, $9.95 paper)

Tuesday's featured guest at the 46th regular monthly meeting of the Springfield Women's Literary Circle was newly published author Helen Lovejoy, wife of our own Rev. Lovejoy.

Ms. Lovejoy read from her best-selling book, "And Then They Took Naps", a novel based on the fantasy lives of certain Springfield housewives.

The session was lively and sometimes heated. An argument broke out when Selma Bouvier stood up and interrupted Ms. Lovejoy, saying, "Well, let's stop pussy-footing around, shall we? I mean, just who *are* the housewives you describe in 'Naps'?"

Ms. Bouvier's challenge touched off a raucous argument among the 23 members present, half of whom joined her call for full disclosure, chanting, "Let's hear the names!"

Chairperson Marjorie Simpson finally restored order by shouting above the noise,"Ladies! Please! I think we can agree there's a little of all of us in every one of these characters. Now, isn't it about time for the lovely cookies baked for us today by Gloria Blaze, uh, I mean Maude Flanders…"?

Next month's meeting will welcome the much-traveled botanist and photographer Lee Maltborn, who will discuss his highly acclaimed

HOUSEWIFE WEEKLY

Beauty Tips Contest!

SIMPLY FILL OUT THE FORM BELOW WITH ALL YOUR FAVORITE, TRIED-AND-TRUE BEAUTY SECRETS! WE ALL HAVE OUR LITTLE MIRACLE FORMULAS AND TOP-SECRET WRINKLE REMEDIES TO KEEP US LOOKING GOOD, SO WHY NOT SHARE YOURS?

1. ~~To remove wrinkles, steep with a yogurt facial treat-meat. BE sure to stir up fruit from bottom!~~

2. To make your eyes look bigger, curl lashes.

3. When in doubt about your hair, tease it!

4. Always clench your teeth when you smile.

5. Gravity is Beauty's enemy number one. Maintain bouyant thoughts

6. For younger-looking skin, lie face down in a mud puddle for 20 minutes

7. Mix your base with orange food coloring for a more "natural" look.

8. Keep your hair looking peppy with static electricity!

9. Instead of drying your hair with a blow dryer, ~~use a cotton candy machine.~~

10. My number one beauty secret a wa

YOU COULD WIN AN ALL-EXPENSE PAID TRIP TO HOUSEWIFE WEEKLY'S BEAUTY HEAD-QUARTERS, A COMPLETE MAKE-OVER AND AN OPPORTUNITY TO BE A "BEFORE" AND "AFTER" MODEL IN THIS MAGAZINE!

Name Ma___
Address ___
Wats___
Spring___
Zip ___ 002__
Phone 555__

I almost sent this in, but the idea of being a "before" just rubbed me the wrong way.

LOST AND FOUND

LOST: Maroon fez, size 3 7/8. Very rare, late 18th century Moroccan headgear. Owner heartsick. Personal identity at stake. REWARD. Contact Jeff at 555-3721.

FOUND: Flower pot-shaped object made of stiff, dark red felt. Seamless, with 8" black tassel attached to bottom. Object was left on bench near bulletin board at Springfield Natural Foods Collective. No reward expected, please. I'd just like to know what this thing is, what it's used for. Call 555-0463.

MISSING

Male cat and father of the offspring of Snowball II. Entire Family distraught. Children growing suspicious. Running out of excuses. If found, please contact the Simpsons at 555 - 8707.

— CLASSIFIED AN

MEETINGS

SPRINGFIELD SPRINGER SPANIEL SOCIETY meets third Wednesday of each month, Order of the Opossum Lodge basement. October 23, hear Lars Dengman, Universith of Malmo. Topic: "New Cholesterol-Free Doggie Donut Lite...Fetch or Forget?"

SPRINGFIELD CLASSICAL HUMMING CHORUS is looking for tenors. Ever find yourself just bursting into the Duh-duh-dun, duh-dun-dun, duh-duh-dun-dun-dun version of Rossini's "William Tell Overture"? Ever yearn to combine your talent with others? Then come to Room 222, Order of the Opossum Lodge, Wed. Oct.23. You could land a part in this year's humming of Holst's "The Planets"!

Something about the father's disappearance left me with an uneasy sense of déjà-vu.

Snowball II, on the other hand, seemed completely unconcerned.

Lisa's second-grade play

FEUD at SQUIRREL HOLLOW

A PLAY IN TWO ACTS

Presented by the *Springfield Elementary Players*

Grandma Checkerberry	Janey Hagstrom
Grandpa Checkerberry	Lewis Jackson
Lilly May	Susan Hegarty
Rufus	Robert DuRee
Ol' "Bugeared" Maloney	Frank Isola
Mayor Quimby	Lisa Simpson
Stage Hands	Bart Simpson
	Nelson Widmar
	Milhouse Light and Magic
Lighting	Carin Berger
Costumes	Terry Castillo
Hair and Make-up	Mrs. Hoover
Directed by	

ACT I: The fur flies when Grandma finds her *go-to-meetin'* dress full of buckshot holes. On Grandpa's advice, she suspects Rufus and tells him so, but Rufus has a darn good alibi. Together, Grandma, Grandpa and Rufus vow to get to the bottom of this.

ACT II: The trail leads straight to Ol' Bugeared Maloney—or does it? Turns out he's got a darn good alibi too. Ol' Bugeared joins the posse, and the four vigilantes keep trying to get to the bottom of this. Finally...Eureka! (Hang onto your seats.)

Bart drew this at age seven...

MY DAD

BART

She was so proud to be cast as the Mayor!

Not a bad likeness, really.

Bart was in charge of lighting

At long last! One of Grandpa's letters finally gets published!

Our trip to Mt. Rushmore!

OCT. 2, 1989   SPRINGFI

SICK AND TIRED

Editor, *Springfield Shopper*,

I am sick and tired of writing angry, blathering letters to you morons and never seeing them in print!

Do you think I do this just to heart myself squawk?

The First Amendment should stand for more than just wasted stationery— paper doesn't grow on trees, you know!

—Grampa Simpson

FEBRUARY 9, 1990

Man nearly Dies in Bizarre Leap over Springfield Gorge

Another 10 ft. and he'd have made it.

Instead, dozens watched in horror as local resident Homer Simpson crashed and fell into the rocky depths of Springfield Gorge yesterday afternoon in impromptu attempt to sail across the familiar landmark on his son's skateboard.

GET WELL SOOO

One of the greatest inventions since the t.v.!

BARTO WAS here

Recipes

PLAN-AHEAD, MAKE-AHEAD CALIFORNIA DIP

1 package onion soup mix
1/2 pint sour cream
Mix.
Chill.
Serve, with Krinkle-Time Potato Chips.

Our trip to Mt. Splashmore!

Visit **MT. SPLASHMORE**

WATER WONDER-LAND!

Xtra-Wet!
Xtra-Splashy!
Xtra-Foamy!

PLEASE DO NOT SWIM NEAR AUTOMATIC SUCTION DRAINS.

WE CANNOT BE RESPONSIBLE FOR CONCUSSIONS, WATER IN THE LUNGS OR FRICTION BURNS.

You may find yourself in a tight situation!

Maggie's first teeth!

I SURVIVED MT. SPLASHMORE!

Homer got stuck *Barely* in the tunnel – which was bad – but it did prompt him to diet – which was good!

NEVER SAY DIET

BECAUSE YOU DESERVE IT!

DIMOXINOL

GUARANTEED!

to return hair to original thickness and length, in most cases…unless we've missed our address.

WARNING: Dimoxinal should not be used unless (1) recommended by a licensed physician (2) purchased by calling a 1-800 number shown on cable television or (3) suggested by a pharmacy cashier wearing a clean, white coat.

DISCLAIMER: KEEP OUT OF REACH OF CHILDREN. No child under the age of 12 be allowed to play with or around this bottle. At no time should a sarcastic-tongued, disrespectful first-born male child be allowed to play with or around this bottle. Follicle Laboratories, Inc. assumes no responsibility for customer's failure to comply with this provision.

TRY THESE OTHER PROVEN FOLLICLE PRODUCTS!
- Gee, Your Lip Looks Hairless!
- Hair-Go Leg Hair Removal Kit
- Big 'n' Fluffy Hair Enhancer
- Hair's-a-Poppin' Hair Plug Home Treatment
- Dimoxinal Plus

Homer and his miraculous hair

The Day After ↱

"Howl of the Unappreciated"
by Lisa Simpson

I saw the best meals of
my generation
destroyed by the madness
of my brother.
My soul carved in slices
by spikey-haired demons.

...ksgiving Cranberry Log

2 cans xtra-jellied
seedless cranberry
sauce
Mint

Open cranberry jellies.
Place (tandem) on
decorative platter.
(be sure to slide out
carefully so jelly remains
in shape of can!)

Add "mint" for "leaves."
Voila!

El Bandito Motel

The year we decided to break with
Thanksgiving tradition and serve pork
chops instead!

with apologies
to the pilgrims.
-L.S.

Lisa's
lovely
cornucopia
centerpiece

Dear Principal Skinner,
Please excuse Bart's absince from school ~~today~~, March 3-5. He stayed home to take care of his mother, who could not use her hands because she burned both of them in a Terrible Kitchen accident, which is why this letter looks like a kid did it.
Sincerely,
Margorie Simpson
March 6th

SPRINGFIELD ELEMENTARY SCHOOL

March 6

Dear Mr. and Mrs. Simpson:

I know I've said this many times before, but this really is the last straw.

Enclosed you will find your son Bartholomew's latest pathetic attempt at forgery. If he thinks he can hoodwink my authority, he's got another think coming.

I'm afraid your son Bartholomew is on a one-way conveyor belt to J.D.H., and I don't mean the Junior Disneyland Hotel. I mean the Juvenile Detention Home!

I am adding another 40 days detention, which brings his total to 462 days.

He will also be required to write on the blackboard 1000 times:

A FORGED EXCUSE IS INEXCUSABLE.

I can only hope you will take even sterner measures of discipline in the privacy of your own home.

Sincerely,

Seymour Skinner
Principal

REPORT CARD
SPRINGFIELD ELEMENTARY SCHOOL

Student: Simpson, Bart

	1st SEM.	2nd SEM.	3rd SEM.
Arithmatic	F	D-	F
Social Studies	D+	F	F+
English	D-	F+	D
History	F	F	D-
Art	F-	D	D+
P.E.	D+	F	F

Comments: Dear Mr. and Mrs. Simpson, As we are painfully aware, Bart is his own worst enemy. Unfortunately, the enemy is winning. Nothing you or I could say or do would make a bit of difference.
With mutual concern,
Ms. Krabappel

From the Desk of
J. Loren Pryor
DISTRICT PSYCHOLOGIST

SUBJECT: Bart Simpson   Age: 10

EVALUATION: Subject exhibits need to draw excessive attention to himself. Confrontational behavior includes attempts at raw humor intended to confuse authority figures and disrupt peer group order.

CONCLUSION: Rotten Little Punk.

SIGNED: J. Loren Pryor

EL BARTO WAS HERE

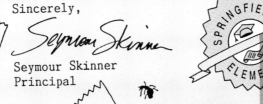

SPRINGFIELD ELEMENTARY
GRADE FOUR
Ms. Krabappel

Ms. Krabappel   Principal Skinner

Merry Xmas!

Maggie

Santa's Little Helper

Snowball II

BART

Homer

The Simpsons

Marge

Lisa

QUICK RECIPE #3

1 MINUTE EGGNOG

Rum (1 pint)

Milk (1 quart)

Eggs (6)

Pour ingredients into a
blender, frappe 30 seconds
and serve at room temperat__
(For housewives on the go--
make ahead of time and chil__

YULE LOG

1 pkg. Yellow Cake Mix
1 can Brown Frosting
Coffee can
gumdrops
parsley

Make cake mix. Pour into
coffee can. Bake 40 min.
Pull out of can (important!)
and frost.

Decorate with gumdrops.

Add parsley for "moss".

My Xmas List

Lisa

A pony

A pony

A pony

A pony

A pony

A pony

A pony

I don't know what I'll do if I don't get a pony this year.

My Xmas List

Homer

- Stealth Bowler
- Coupon Booklet for Barney's Bowlarama
- NO TIES, please
- Case of Duff
- Mambo Refresher Course

Merry Xmas from the
DEPARTMENT OF MOTOR VEHICLES

Free Ice Scraper to all Organ Donors before December 31st. (Limit 1 per customer).

My Xmas List

BART

tattoo - secret combo padlock for my bedroom door.
...yo-yo
...cer - MOON SHOES
...ot
...um - Electric RAZOR
...ra - RADIO
...ull active Man walkie
...rusty talkie
...t-shirt
...ace Mutants - POP GUN

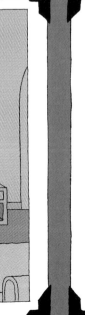

Xmas morning, 6:03 A.M.

Xmas morning, 6:07 A.M.

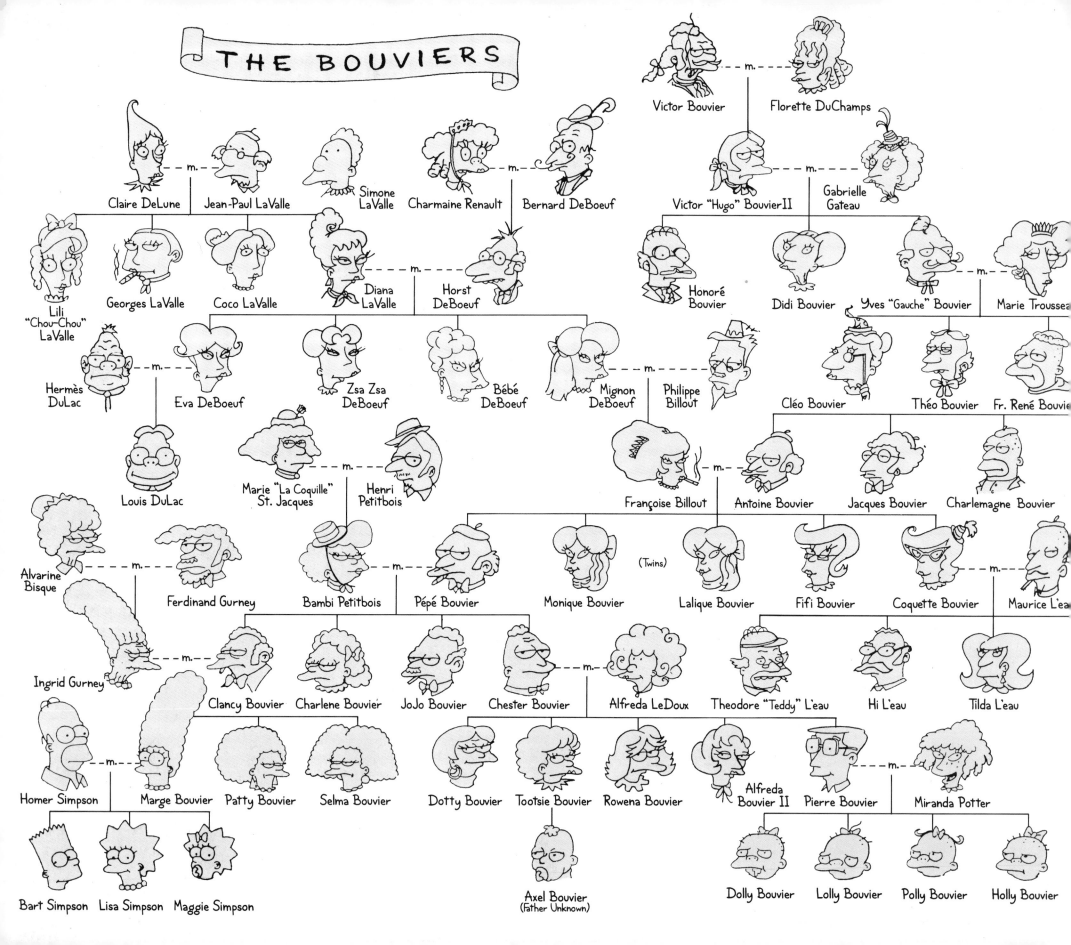